THE
POSSESSION

KNOW THE GHOST CONDITION
AND
OVERCOME NEGATIVE SPIRITUAL INFLUENCE

RYUHO OKAWA

HS PRESS

Contents

2

About Something Supernatural

3

The Ghost Condition

Afterword 97

* The lectures were conducted in English.

Preface

It's already 39 years since I had my first spiritual awakening. The title of this book, "The Possession", has been a very important theme for a long time. In many cases, what people think they are doing of their own free will is actually influenced by the phenomenon of spiritual possession. This means it's also quite difficult to judge between good and bad in the legal meaning.

There is the law of the same wavelengths, and usually the person who is possessed and the spirit who is possessing both have a similar tendency of the soul. If this is the case, then it means that you can choose your "spiritual friend" by making the effort of changing yourself.

A life of blaming other people and the environment is empty. Go closer toward the light. You can find various hints scattered inside this book.

Ryuho Okawa
Master & CEO of Happy Science Group
Jan. 28, 2020

1

The Possession

Lecture given on September 24, 2019
Special Lecture Hall, Happy Science, Japan

1

This World is Influenced By Another World

"The Possession" is An important Buddha's Truth

Today's title is, "The Possession," like the theme of a movie. [*Laughs.*] So, it's a little funny and difficult for me, but I'll try.

How do you feel about the sound of "The Possession"? Almost all of you may feel that, "Oh, it's terrible," or "Oh, incredible," or "I never want to see such kind of paranormal phenomena," or like that. Almost 90 percent of you will want to escape from this situation or this kind of movie titled, *The Possession*. I'm afraid so, but this is very important; a very, very important Buddha's Truth.

Almost all of you might be feeling that the possession is a bad meaning, but in the true meaning, it's not so. The possession is the common phenomenon we watch every day. We, I mean the humankind who are living in this world with a body, cannot see anything else without a body; if it's a human or an animal, it doesn't matter. We, humankind, can see only the figure of the bodies, or if it's not the body, you can see things, the material things. So, you are apt to think that this world is composed of bodies and things, and that's all.

But in reality, our real world is made up of spiritual entities, I mean spiritual beings. Of course, one is the spirits of humankind, but another one is the spirits of animals, and in addition to that, exceptional spiritual beings which are made by God. We, who are living in this three-dimensional world, cannot see, but there are a lot of such kinds of spiritual beings in the Real World. For example, you cannot see dragons in this world nowadays, but when you go back to another world, you can easily see dragons. One type is dragons who are flying over the sky, and other dragons are on the dark side and, of course, killing a lot of people or animals. This is the reality.

This world is the inside of a soccer ball

So, this lecture's main points are, "What is the possession?" and "What's the influence of the possession to you?" So, we are living in this three-dimensional world, but this three-dimensional world is not the world of bodies and things only. It also means this world gets a lot of effects from another world.

We are living in the spiritual world. In this spiritual world, there is floating some kind of ball-like universe. It's like a soccer ball- or basketball-like ball. Within this ball, we call this small inner world as the three-dimensional world and the phenomenal world. And we just think that the world is limited in this ball only, but there are a lot of lives outside of this ball.

For example, if this ball is a soccer ball, you can throw it or you can kick it. And how will the small people who are living inside of the soccer ball feel about that? "Oh, there comes a gigantic power outside of our universe," or "I feel we are flying through the air, but indeed there is nothing happening." This is the recognition of the Real World. So, the main point is, "The existence or entity of another world can have influence on us, the earthly-being people." But almost 99 percent of us cannot feel any such kind of influence from another world.

A curious story of Obon

Sometimes, you will hear, for example, the channelers' saying, or abnormal activity or incredible activity that your friends or other people are chatting about.

For example, when I was in my childhood,

maybe around 10 or so, it was the middle of August maybe—it's *Obon* of Japan; it means during the days, I mean, the one week of the middle of August, our ancestors come back from another world and can see their descendants, I mean the children or grandchildren or their relatives. This is Japanese *Obon*. It might have been around when I was 10 years old. My mother and father and my aunt who was a writer were gathering around the living room, and they were talking about my ancestor, it's the grandmother who died almost six years before that time. My grandmother died in Tokyo, and almost the same time, she came back to Kawashima Town, my birthplace in Tokushima Prefecture, Shikoku, and then the back door of our dining room opened about one foot or so. There was no one, of course, at that time. And, they said that my grandmother came back. After that, on that night or so, they said they heard that, yeah, indeed she died at the time of the automatic opening of our back door of the dining room. I've been brought up hearing that kind of story a lot.

2

The Possession Means Souls of Another World Make Influence On You

You can see dead people in your dreams

But today, I must be focused on the theme of "The Possession." So, to teach about the possession, we must recognize that, "In reality, we are souls, and we have one soul in one body. And, after our death, we are going to another world, it's heaven or hell, or the spiritual world between these two."

So, when people leave this world, we cannot see him or her anymore, but someone will appear in your dreams. You can see dead people during your sleeping at night. All of you might have such kind of dreams of people who are not living in this world anymore, but you cannot believe that you met ghosts at that time because in your dream, you can see other people who are living in this world, also. So, you are prone to think that it's just made-up dreams by our brain activities. Doctors will say so.

But I dare say, if you see clear and sometimes colored dreams, when you see them, you, I mean your soul, will experience out-of-the-body experience, and in another world, you usually meet the people who are already dead. And, when you wake up, sometimes you remember about the dead people, but some of them are translated into memory of living people, like your friend or living family or teacher or students of the school or people who live in your neighborhood. So, you cannot believe that you've met the dead during your night dream or nightmare. But indeed, you all have spiritual power in you, and if you focus on your dream, you can intentionally meet people who have passed away, your relative or your family. I can say so.

The possession means a spirit wants to Say something, has attachment, Or seeks help from you

So, I just want to say, the possession means the souls outside of this world come back to this world, and commonly affect or make influence on you because those entities want to say something to you or have some attachment to you or are drowning in the dark sea or river in another world and seeking help from you. Or, they want to teach you that, "Oh, one of your relatives or your parent or your grandfather or grandmother is in evil situation now, and you, the family left, should help us or help me." They want to say like that because they don't know how to save themselves.

Some people have a custom to go to church and listen carefully to the priest's teaching of the Testament, but that priest also cannot understand another world correctly, so they cannot teach you "what is the possession." So, you only can understand the meaning of possession through horror movies or so, and this is some kind of impression and a terrible experience. No one can totally teach you about this phenomenon.

3

Your Fate is Influenced By Other Spirits

A chain of misfortunes
Could be because of the possession

So, I teach you the possession. In another way, the possession means the ghost possession, the ghosts who left this world and who cannot find their future way where they should go. They cannot be guided by their guardian angel and are wandering around this world. They attach to school or family or their company or their job, and they are walking around their friends or among their colleagues. And, they are seeking some kind of exit, I mean, a person who can feel something from their inspiration. It's very difficult for them to find such kind of person. So, if they cannot find such able person, they are apt to attach to their child or husband or wife or parents.

We usually feel that because of bad accidents. If there occurs some bad accident, for example, a car accident or your child is injured at school or you get fired, or like that, something evil, two or three or four occurs, at that time, you feel, "Some irregularities are happening around me. What's that? It might be my father who passed away three months ago. Is he now in heaven or not?" Some of you can ask about him at the temple or shrine or Happy Science branch, and teachers of that kind of temple or shrine or branch would tell you, "It might be so. Your father is at a loss now, and he's around you every day. Maybe you have experienced a nightmare that something terrible happened to you, and you already met your dead father in your dream." "Yeah, it's true. But what can I do about that?" You will maybe ask.

Who is influencing you?

The answer is—this is very important—the answer is, you can live your life through your own way of thinking and activity. But in another meaning, it's not you, only, that will make your fate. You are influenced by other spiritual beings, your deceased relatives, or in some meaning, you will meet devils or demons in your life. It means they can get some kind of job because of you. Or, some angels will give you inspirations.

Please think about that. Concentrate on your mind, and think about that. "Is this my relatives' souls' influence, or the influence which comes from evils, I mean just straying souls or bad souls or demon-like souls or angels?" If you can see yourself from the standpoint of another person, you can find the answer to this question.

If you can be an independent person, you will make your efforts and want to get through your difficulties. In some meaning, it's OK. You are a strong person. And, in this situation, you will get the inspiration from the heavenly world, maybe heavenly person or angels.

But if you felt that, "I'm in bad condition now, and I feel difficulties in my daily work," or "I feel difficulties in my family matters," or "I don't think it's good because I'm not so healthy," and "I'm not so good in the emotional meaning, and this will come from the evil side of the spiritual world," if you think so, that is the main problem of the possession.

4

How Can You Be Protected By Saintly Power?

You can see the power of angels At Happy Science

I mean, the possession—it's, of course, the influence of the souls, but if the influence comes from your happy deceased relatives from heaven, it's a not-so-big matter. They just want to give you your hope or want to make your future brighter, and angels also do, so it doesn't matter. Of course, angels can possess you, but it means they want to direct the right way for you, so it doesn't matter.

The point is, the possession of evil spirits, especially the demon-like existences, or Satan, itself. In this case, sometimes you need exorcism, but there are few real exorcists in this world, so it's very difficult. You can find that we succeed in exorcism or not. Even the Catholic Church or Vatican cannot do effectively regarding exorcism. We, Happy Science, do a lot regarding exorcism, and we have a lot of helpers from heaven and higher spiritual realms, I mean the seventh spiritual realm—Bodhisattva Realm, it means—or the eighth dimensional realm, Tathagata Realm, and the ninth dimensional realm, where there live the saviors like Jesus Christ or Gautama Buddha or Moses or Maitreya, or like that.*

We, Happy Science, precisely understand the system and the powers of higher spirits. So, if you go to our Happy Science branch instead of going to a Christian church, there you can see the real spirits of angels or spiritual power of higher existences. Finally, you will receive the super power of El Cantare† at the branch office or *shoja* of Happy Science.

---

* See *The Nine Dimensions* (New York: IRH Press, 2012).

† The Supreme God of the Earth Spirit Group; God of the Earth who has guided humanity since the beginning of Earth and who was also involved in the Creation of the universe. The *honzon* (object of worship) at Happy Science. See *The Laws of the Sun* (New York: IRH Press, 2018).

I mean, firstly, if you find that you have some contact with such kind of dismayed people, it means, for example, people who dropped dead recently and don't know about their death, or evil spirits who want to disturb your sacred activities like *dendo* (missionary work) or saving people, yeah, it indeed will occur now and in the near future.

Believe in El Cantare and the Three Treasures, And you can be protected

If you get more power than as it is, sometimes evil spirits will be replaced by demons or Satan-like great spiritual powers, and it will disturb your mission and sometimes attack the branch chief or lecturer. Yes, indeed, it will occur, but you can cut the relation between such kind of bad spiritual beings and you. If you have enough belief in El Cantare and you have faith in the Three Treasures, I mean the Buddha, Buddha's law, and the Sangha, meaning the members of Happy Science, you can be protected by saintly power from heaven and from this earth.

So, never fight against evil by yourself. Please rely on Happy Science group and the lecturers of Happy Science and teachings of Happy Science, and finally, of course, please rely on El Cantare. No one can defeat El Cantare in this world and in another world because El Cantare was and is the origin of the human souls of this Earth.

Even the (souls of) Satans were made by El Cantare. They sometimes did bad deeds and have self-preservation too much. They made rebellion against gods and are now on the dark side, and are gathering their disciples of bad, evil side, like Darth Vader's disciples. But their powers and their groups are very limited to just the underside of the fourth dimensional world and this world, the three-dimensional world only, because they are very much attached to worldly matters and want to get the flesh, I mean the body. Indeed, they want to be reborn into this world as a human, but no one can be reborn into this world from hell because if they could, hell would be empty now and there would be a lot of bad guys in this world, day by day.

5

The Rule of Possession

People cannot be reborn from hell

Angels are very lucky and comfortable in heaven, so they sometimes come down to this world to save people or to make good efforts to promote this world, but usually, they are living in heaven.

But people who are suffering from the very dreadful atmosphere of hell, they want to be reborn into this earth, but it's prohibited. They need promise and permission of the people who are given the power to make them reborn. It's the special people, chosen people who give them permission. But they cannot get any permission, so they only can possess this world's people.

Speaking ill and blaming
Will attract the possession

There is a rule, of course. The people who are living in this world, their way of thinking is wavering, day by day or all day long in a day. But all people have a tendency. Usual people sometimes think good things and sometimes think bad things, but people who make reflection every day can make their mind in tune with the heavenly world. But people who cannot reflect on their lives and people who cannot pray for God or angels only think about bad things and have attachment to evil things or evil sayings.

They usually say bad things to other people, "That is Dad" or "That is Mom who made me unhappy," or "That is the bad teacher who made me unhappy," or "Bad friends, they made me unhappy," or "The school was bad," or their company was a very bad condition to work in every day. So, they have a tendency to blame the responsibility on other people or conditions or environment.

Of course, the national environment, for example, the prime minister is bad, or so. It contains that kind of political situation, also. In some meaning, it's true, but in another meaning, even if the prime minister were bad indeed, it will never save you. You can choose the way you get through your evil situation in this world. So, I have been recommending such kind of spiritual attitude.

6

Do What You Can to Change Yourself

Change your mind and give love to others

But if you are already too late to save yourself from the spiritual attack of evil spirits, please think that, "The concentration will make your direction of your mind." Please check your mind, the direction. "Which direction does it indicate?" or "Does it indicate heaven or hell?" or "Am I occupied by evil words only or not?" If you can do something by yourself, do it first.

But at the same time, read my books and pray for your guardian spirit or the guiding spirits of Happy Science and please make friends with our followers. In your branch office, there is a spiritual screen surrounding the branch, and it will make you stronger and help you to make a wall to bad spirits. So, choose one of two; one direction, the good direction.

If you have been living unhappy or self-concentrated or self-preserved type living, please change your mind and please give your love to others. You may have the compassion for others. In other words, please feel mercy from heaven. And, if you can shed some kind of mercy from you to miserable people or unfortunate people, you are the aid of angels, so it's very much important.

Have a good connection with sacred people, And be familiar with the textbooks of Happy Science

The total conclusion of "The Possession" is, if you want to make the evil spirits leave you, please have a good connection with the sacred part of the world and sacred people, and be familiar with the textbooks of our teachings. Then, you can change yourself with the aid of other good people. So, we have a stress on strong *dendo* now. We need to help others, and at the same time, we need the powers to help us and to spread these teachings in the world.

So, I just want to get rid of the possession of evil spirits every day. People who are reading my books every day and people who are praying for me every day or people who are doing good things to others will be protected from evil influences and can be free from the possession.

That is the easy explanation regarding the possession. Could you follow me enoughly? OK. Then, if you have one question.

Q: What are some checkpoints to know we are possessed?

QUESTIONER

As humans living on this earth, we find it difficult to realize that we are under possession when we are actually possessed. Even if other people advise us, in most of cases, it is hard to accept. So, could you please teach us some checkpoints or a simple way to know that we are possessed?

RYUHO OKAWA

OK. If you are possessed by something evil, people surrounding you are apt to feel something bad from you. So, people will want to keep a distance from you, and sometimes speak ill of you or change their minds. "He or she was my friend, but now I feel very cool or sad emotions from them," or "They don't want to be a friend of mine," or sometimes, if you work, people around you will say that, "Don't touch this matter, you don't have enough capability," like that.

In some meaning, indeed, it's true, maybe. But in another meaning, if you feel that is not correct or right, in that case, something evil is attached to you and making some kind of circumstances around you, a bad influence around you. In some meaning, people have channeler-like feeling. Almost all of them have some kind of channeler-like feeling.

So, if you find that, please concentrate on your real mind, and make yourself and keep yourself in peace and peace of mind. "Can I find peace of mind in me or not?" or "Did I say something evil to other people?" or "Did I act something in contrary to Happy Science teachings?" or "Am I proud of myself too much?" or "Do I have too much pride or not?" Please go deep inside you and find the reason.

If you never find such kind of reason, just be patient and keep silence and read our teachings and just do good things in your life. Never be proud too much about what you said. As Jesus teaches you, don't let it know to your left hand what your right hand did. For example, people sometimes make a great mistake in their peak activity or peak period. You are doing your best, and you want to receive praise from other people. At the same time, you are apt to dig your hole to throw yourself into it.

So, never think too much about evil things and other people's bad sayings, and instead concentrate on your mind and peace of mind. Please concentrate on your prayer for God, and wait time to let the bad people or influence of the evil spirits leave you. You may need three months or six months, maybe, but in those months, you can get through. You'll get through your difficulties and look at your brighter side in that period.

But if you have too much ego in you and look at the brighter side only, it's not correct. You must accept other people's criticisms and change your mind. You need to. So, it's very difficult, but it's your way of promotion in enlightenment. I think so.

2

About Something Supernatural

Lecture given on September 20, 2016
Special Lecture Hall, Happy Science, Japan

Q1: What is the most powerful weapon against evil spirits?

RYUHO OKAWA

OK. Is there any question about something supernatural through your experience or your knowledge or something you want to know?

QUESTIONER

Recently, I watched several movies about exorcists, and in the movies, Catholic priests used, for example, holy water, the Bible, and so on. So, what is the most important and powerful weapon against evil spirits?

The main point is
The spiritual power of the exorcist, not the tools

RYUHO OKAWA

The question is a question. These weapons are effective or not is a secret of Catholicism, so I cannot say clearly about that. Because if I say, "It doesn't work," it means losing of the Catholicism, and if I say, "It's effective," the Satans will laugh at that. So, it's very difficult for me to answer. But even the Bible and the holy water and the sacred cross, these are not so effective for the evil spirits, demons or Satans, because they know these things very well. So, it's not fearful for them to use such kind of tools.

The main point is the power of the person who uses these tools. It's one of the symbols, I think; it's a symbol of God or God's power or the miracle power of gods. So, the main point is the real spiritual power of the person who uses these tools. It means whether the priest or the father of Catholicism has made great efforts to acquire such kind of supernatural spiritual power or not, through his learning from the Bible or through his concentration on something, for example, praying on someone's curing of illness or praying on God. This concentration is very essential.

And, his experience is also very essential. How has he gotten through his whole life, especially from the time when he made up his mind to work for the sake of God? So, if there is some supernatural power, these things, the Holy Bible or holy water or holy cross, will seem to be essential and effective to some evil spirits. They will fear these tools. But in reality, it's from the sacred power of the person who conducts the exorcism.

Q2: What happens when belief brings miracles?

QUESTIONER

I'd like to ask about miracles in Happy Science. We, believers, at Happy Science temple or shoja and at home, pray to God, learn Master's lecture or practice self-reflection. Sometimes miracles happen. It means healing illness, overcoming sufferings. What happens at these moments in the spiritual meaning or supernatural meaning?

More than 99 percent of this world Is built on material rules

RYUHO OKAWA

OK. You want to know the meaning of miracles, like that. But to tell the truth, the truth that you humans have lives with you, is the true miracle. I think so. Through your eyes, you cannot see anything about soul or spiritual being or something divine, so it is easy for you all to believe in materialism. It is to live as it is, to just believe that which you can touch or give or throw or like that. Material things are easily to be believed to exist in this world, so everyone who can see believes the existence of such kinds of goods or existences. Even the person who has eye troubles, can touch such kinds of things. He can believe the existence of those beings.

But when we talk about the spiritual beings, soul, or mind, or something like that, people easily resist to believe such kind of entity, I mean the existence of a spiritual being. I understand because this is the world which was built in such regulation, I mean in such law of materialism. This world, I mean the three-dimensional world is built on the material rules, more than 99 percent. This world is built upon materialism, but only one percent you can see or experience or feel something exceptional.

For example, you can think that you, yourselves, are made up from flesh, I mean material components, but even scientists within you can feel something different. It might be only one percent or so.

A SUPERNATURAL EXPERIENCE 1
Seeing the deceased in your dreams

But he, himself, cannot be a complete, extreme materialist because, for example, we can see dreams while we are lying at night. In the dreams, you can see a lot of quite different experiences. Some are, for example, you can see dead parents or grandparents or your dead son or daughter, it is unusual and uncommon. So, if you experience such kind of discovery several times, you are sometimes apt to think that you can meet your lost son or daughter or your lost parents in another world. "It's a meaning of dream," you are apt to think like that.

Usually, in the world of business, you don't say such kind of things. But after your business time, sometimes you and your family or your friends talk about such things. If you can believe in him, believe his friendship, or "You are the man of truth," if they think like that, then they can hear from you such kind of things. They can say that, "I believe you because you are a man of truth. You don't say a lie," so they can share your beliefs, for example. It's one thing.

A SUPERNATURAL EXPERIENCE 2
A daydream-like feeling

Another thing is, you, yourself, experience such kind of supernatural thing while you are awake. It means in the daytime you sometimes see something which cannot be explained if you think that there is nothing other than material things in this world. For example, you can foresee someone's death or you can foresee or foretell the accident of your family or family's car, or sometimes you can get some inspiration from heaven that your aunt is dead or not.

It's not a dream, not a daydream. It's a daydream-like experience, but you sometimes feel like that. While you are studying or while you are doing business, you feel the existence of, for example, your aunt or uncle who lives long distance away, I mean not close to you at hand. But you felt something spiritual. "It might be my aunt or my uncle who just came into my room," or "I heard a voice of my uncle just now" or like that. These kinds of experiences are usual and common, and maybe 60 or 70 percent of the people, if they are permitted to say the truth, they will agree that, "I felt something at that time." They can say like that.

Or, in another time, it's not exactly the daytime, but usually at night, you can see someone who passed away already but exactly as he or she was living, that kind of style. So, this is an experience of ghost or spirit, but someone can experience this fact.

So, people usually think like that under their surface consciousness, but they can assume this truth while they are attending at the meeting of the church or some kind of spiritual circle or like that. So, it's very difficult, but there are a lot of chances for them to acknowledge such kind of supernatural experience.

A SUPERNATURAL EXPERIENCE 3
Being cured of an illness

And, sometimes you can share the miracles with other people. For example, Mother Teresa was recently admitted to be a saint because after her death, there really occurred two miracles, which means when a person who believes in her prayed on curing someone, at that time, the difficult illness cured; and there were two samples. That's enough for the agreement to be a saint.

In our Happy Science, it's not so unusual a case. Every day, I've heard that illness is cured in every case by dint of the power of prayer or by dint of power of reading *Shoshinhogo* (*The True Words Spoken By Buddha*)* or by dint of reading my books or by dint of watching my videos, like that. So, I can be more than a saint. I think so. It's uncountable because hundreds or thousands of miracles have already occurred in Happy Science. So, this is a result of our movement.

The stronger your El Cantare-belief, The more miracles will occur

The most important thing when we make a miracle or let the people feel a miracle—it's a belief. It is the most powerful weapon for miracles. So, if you

* The fundamental sutra of Happy Science that is given to all its members. The words were written by the ninth-dimensional Gautama Buddha consciousness, which is one of the branch spirits of El Cantare.

believe deeply, you can do everything, even in this world. I think so.

And, at the time, you must know about the meaning of belief. This belief is the belief through El Cantare and his essential existence as a main consciousness of the worldwide spiritual being. It has a lot of names, and in every time and every area, people say it's God or Buddha, like that. You can acquire that spiritual original being, the spiritual real entity, through El Cantare-belief.

So, if you have El Cantare-belief and you believe in it stronger and stronger, there will occur a lot of miracles now, and from the day after, tomorrow, or in the near future or like that. A lot of books which I have written explain enoughly about the system of cause and effect of the miracle, so please study these books and it will help you to make a new miracle. I hope so.

Q3: How can we protect ourselves from evil spirits?

QUESTIONER

People who are possessed by evil spirits can expel them by participating in a ritual prayer, or kigan, however, they are soon possessed again because of their weakness or their spiritual connection to the evil spirits. How can we prevent them from coming back and protect ourselves?

Check the connection between the person Who is possessed and the evil spirit

RYUHO OKAWA

It's a difficult question. Even Catholicism, I mean the selected people who can conduct an exorcism within Catholicism, I mean the chosen priests, fathers, cannot answer your question. It's very difficult.

They will conduct an exorcism, but the only conclusion is, as they learned from the Latin Bible, they ask some supernatural being within the target, I mean the person who is possessed by something, they just ask that entity, "Who are you?" "Say your name." And, if the Satan or someone says their real name, after that, the exorcists say, "In the name of God" or "In the name of Jesus Christ, I will punish you and persecute you and command, never come back to this body," they say like that. That's the conclusion. And, sometimes the exorcists conquer and the happy end will come.

But I've seen many films, and in almost 80 percent or 90 percent of the films, Satans got victories and exorcists were ruined by them, sometimes committed suicide at that time. It's when the power of evil spirits surpasses the power of exorcist. So, it's very difficult.

At that time, not only the power of exorcist is estimated, but also the connection between the person who is possessed by an evil spirit and the evil spirit itself. The strength of connection is essential. If this connection is very strong, it's very difficult for the exorcist to dispel such kind of Satan. It means, as you know, the wavelength of the soul; if the person who is possessed by an evil spirit or Satan had lived an evil lifetime, he or she has already been contaminated in the spiritual meaning. So, this kind of contamination cannot be washed out easily.

Black, for example. A human's mind is like a white sheet when he or she comes to this world, but after the person lives for 20 or 30 years, the white sheet changes its color, like brown or black or another; for example, red. If the color... I'll use "color" in the context of wavelengths, for example, the tendency of the soul; for example, he likes blood. It means to kill people or to kill animals or like that. Her or his mind's sheet is red, and there comes the red color devil, I mean the devil who seek for blood of humans or blood of animals or like that. Their combination is very strong, so it's difficult even for a priest to conquer such kind of tendency.

Remake your character through
The teachings, contemplation, and reflection

In this situation, before we conduct the exorcism, we need some teaching for that person. For example, please teach that person, what is justice, or what is good and what is bad. How was your life when you were born in this world, and till this day? What is your life? Please reflect on that matter and change the mind through contemplation.

Contemplation is some kind of focusing while you are in the relaxed mood. It's contemplation. At that time, through contemplation, you can reflect upon yourself, and you can receive some kind of God's light from heaven. It will be helpful for you to start a new life. At the beginning of that kind of new life, when exorcism adds power to her or him, it will be helpful.

So, the main point is, exorcism is the occasional case. It is useful, but the common sense or common usual spiritual status is very essential. So, the main point is, after the exorcism, the person can get some key to open the door to another world, I mean the heavenly world or not, is the key point. So, if the person has more belief in that doctrine or the spirituality or the religion, and can remake their own character into a spiritual one or a religious character who seek for God every day, it will protect such kind of person from being possessed again and again by Satan.

An exorcist must be humble

In this point, I have a lot of experience, so I want to say that, if the person who experiences such kind of exorcism sometimes misunderstand herself or himself that, "I am the chosen person or selected person from others because some kind of miracle appeared around me," this is the most dangerous situation.

So, I just want to say, "Be humble," I mean, think that your this-world-self is small, and admire the power of God. It's OK. But if you think that your power is very strong and "occasionally, the divine power comes down to me," if you think like that, it's very difficult. You are already under the control of Satan, so be careful.

It must be the same as the case of the priest. If he believes in his power too much and thinks little of the power of God, he will fail again. In the near future, he will be at the mercy of, under the free will of devil or something, so be careful. Humility is very important. Humility and small efforts, day by day, are very important. I think so.

Q4: How should we think about exorcism?

QUESTIONER

I'd like to ask about the common problem in Happy Science. Actually, we are disciples of El Cantare, and we learned that our life is soul training, but sometimes we need to, for example, defeat other people's evil spirits in shoja or shibu as a believer or as a staff. However, we are sometimes humble, so we are lacking in confidence to fight against evil spirits.

For example, humility makes us feel like, "We are not connected to El Cantare completely. I have no confidence in my power." Also, I've heard that in the early days of Happy Science, when Master saw a staff conducting exorcism in shibu or shoja, Master said, "Oh, nothing happened. Oh, it didn't work." I've heard such experience. Such thing is very shocking to us. So, I'd like to ask Master if there are phases of training about exorcism, or can we train our power like muscle exercise?

Not all priests succeed in exorcism

RYUHO OKAWA

There are two billion Christian people in the world, but official exorcists are very limited, maybe several hundred or so. In America, maybe within 50 or so. So, two billion people, two billion believers, but we have hundreds of priests who can make exorcism. But not all of them succeed in their conducts. Some are made to fail by devils and lose their belief in God, or Jesus Christ, and become the prey of evil spirits, I mean the tools of evil spirits. And, on the contrary to their former life, they spread the disbelief to churches or Vatican or like that, so it's very difficult. So, even the Vatican sometimes wants to conceal the conduct of exorcism because it's easy to fail. If they fail, or someone fails in dispelling the evil spirits from some person, it equally means defeat of the church.

So, even in Happy Science, there are lot of *shukke* (renunciant staff) members, but not all of them can have enough power and can learn enoughly my teachings, and of course, their beliefs are quite different, I think. In our early days, their studying of the law was very lower level, and they wanted to see a *gensho*, it means the phenomenon of spiritual activities. They had much concern about that spiritual conduct.

But when they are astonished by such deed, they soon forget about it after one week or one month or one year. And, they come back to their daily life and think that, "The person of miracle is a same man like me." He usually thinks so. So, this is quite contrary to our hope.

Attachment to material is the cause of hell

And, a miracle sometimes doesn't occur. It has many reasons, but this world belongs to hell. It's what Gautama Siddhartha, Buddha, told more than 2,500 years ago. I cannot say it's true or not.

But this world is under the strong control of hell, it's true. Even the angels cannot live in this world easily because the common sense of this world is quite contrary to that of heaven, such kind of heavenly sense.

So in truth, this is the false world. In this world, you see a lot of things, but these phenomena are false or mirage or something like that. The life after your passing away, the next life, is the real life. It's a teaching of Buddha, but no one can believe easily this teaching.

But to tell the truth, this world is very difficult to control because this earthly world is a material world, and the attachment to material is the origin of the starting point of hell. We have souls and our own nature is a spiritual one, but we are apt to think that we are material beings. This is the starting point to make hell and to go to hell or like that.

And this point, the attachment to materials, it's a weak point, and it's the target point of Satans to lure human beings and make or show illusions to them. "Yeah. Truly, truly. This world, this material world, is essential, and this material world is real. You are living in the real world. Another world is false. No one can return from another world. So, this world is the real world. This world is a limited world, and your life is limited. Please believe in us Satans. So, you must live this short life comfortably and in luxury, and think about yourself only. This is your life, your limited life; your limited 60 or 70 or 40 years' life. So, you must live for your own sake." This is the teaching of the devils.

A miracle is an exceptional occurrence

In this world, a miracle is an exceptional one, so if you use the percentage of the occurrence of a miracle, it will be very few. I think so. Even in the Lourdes of south France, there are millions of pilgrims from all over the world, but the churches or the Vatican authority admitted as miracles only 100 cases or so. So, this percentage is very small. For example, if they have had one million pilgrims, but there occurred one miracle case, its percentage is very small, so people cannot easily believe such kind of miracle. It's quite exceptional.

So, we must be strong against these things. When people leave this world, they will be separated from other people, and some are destined to go to heaven, but others are destined to go to hell. Such kind of people who have a lot of attachment and lured a lot to this world are invited to hell. These people cannot be saved easily by such kind of miracle.

Angels are usually working every day, but a miracle is a very precious one, so they use the miracle only in an effective case because in this world, there is one rule, the three-dimensional rule. No one can change this rule, but with God's mercy, sometimes there occurs the violation of this law of this world, and people can get, how do I say, an awakened experience in that case.

So, pure people should have such kind of attitude or mind to believe purely the experience or the fact or miracle within them because it's an exceptional one. No one can easily cure illness because you, human beings, should cure usual illness at the hospital nowadays. There are a lot of people who are suffering from illness at hospitals. Maybe millions of people are there, and people who are working for hospitals, for example, doctors and nurses, are using their lives for curing such kind of people. It is a common way. It is admitted by God. Human beings must do something good for others. This is one kind of occupation, so it's good.

This world is a training school of souls

But you must know that all the people who are living in this world must leave this world. Maybe by next century. So, if you think that a miracle is how to cure successfully or not, in this standpoint, you can say devils usually have victories because all the people are destined to be killed by some kind of natural diseases or other accidents or like that. No one can live more than 120 years old nowadays. So, in this case only, if you think that success means "living long in this world," if you think like that, gods will usually lose in the fighting with devils.

But this is not true. This world is just the training course, as you said. This is a training school of souls. So, we must leave this world, but through these several decades or 100 years' life, we must learn something in this world. And, in this world only, angels and a person of devil-to-be can live within the same country or nation. So, this is the quite different experience for the people.

But we must leave this world. It means the person of angel must leave this world and go back to the world of angels, and people who did bad things go down to hell. So, they cannot make friends with each other every day, but in this world only, they can meet. This is the discipline. This is the training.

This is the severe, severe training. But in this world only, we can learn what is love, what is evil, what is justice, what is the aim to live. So, don't hesitate to live this undecided or wavering or unsettled world. It is for your own sake. You can learn a lot from this difficult world. I think so.

3

The Ghost Condition

Lecture given on September 27, 2019
Special Lecture Hall, Happy Science, Japan

1

The Soul Lives On
Even After Death

The ghost condition is
The preparation for your departure

Today, I'll give you a lecture about "The Ghost Condition." The theme is very curious, but no one can say about the ghost condition. Of course, all of you can be ghosts, so there is no condition in this meaning, but I want to teach you about what comes after your death.

As you already know, man is mortal, so your lives are limited. You may die today or tomorrow or one year or five years, 10 years or 50 years later, I don't know exactly. We have a lot of prayers for healing or exorcism, and we can get God's light from heaven and sometimes survive for a while or several years or more than that. I hope all of you can enjoy and have enough hope for the future because of your good deeds, or, you can do a lot of great missions, and as the result, you can leave this world in an easy way and go to the heavenly world and join in angels' group. I hope so.

But the ghost condition is different for every person. So, this is the preparation for your departure. If you are young or not is not so important. The departure time depends on each fate.

The Truth about life and death

So, I'll teach you the thinking, "How to be after your death." This is today's main theme.

You all already have souls in you. This is the starting point, so I ask you, please believe in this truth. If you don't have any soul, you are just a machine-like existence, so your death is just disorder of your machine or just your emptiness in the meaning of life energy.

But I have discovered another world and the truth of the human life, and it started in 1981. So, this is 38 years from that time or more than that, and I published more than 2,500 books including translation to foreign languages. I made about 3,000 lectures* regarding life and death and the world phenomena on, of course, the intelligence from heaven or hell. You can receive some kind of information from another world.

Most important thing is to read revelations from God or Buddha, and the next is to read about the guardian spirit or guiding spirit of saints or famous people who did a lot in the history of human lives. I also make a lecture like this one. This is just the teaching of your Master. If you have confusion in what you believe, you can make your understanding in tune with my lectures.

I receive from a lot of assistant souls of higher position. Some of them are Japanese gods or

---

* At the time of the lecture. As of January, 2020, the author has published over 2,600 books and has given over 3,000 lectures.

other gods of foreign countries, or sometimes I receive revelations from space people, but all the revelations from the heavenly world are with my agreement and are regarded as one of my opinions, so this is another important thing.

So, teaching is important and the interview with other souls from heaven or hell is just your reference, I want to say, or not only reference but also a proof of existence of souls. So, there are differences in their characters.

2

The First Confusion After Death

Imagine if you were to die tomorrow

OK, then. "The Ghost Condition." Please imagine that you, for example, if you die tomorrow, what will happen? Imagine, what will happen to you? You will think about your job, and of course, you will think about your family and how to let them live, or how to manage your company or your followers. You will think a lot about that.

And, with this, you must think about yourself. "Oh, this is my last day. Is it enough for me? Did I work enoughly or not?" It's very difficult for you because no one can say "enough." If you can say, "Oh, it's enough" when you die, you are a great person, I think, or just an ordinary person, I don't know exactly. But if you can say, "It's enough" in the spiritual meaning, if you can say like that, it's preferable.

So, every day, you must think about your death. Is it OK for you to leave this earth? If you think it's not enough, you have something left for the next day or the day after tomorrow. You must do what you must do first. This is important.

No one can hear what you want to say

After your death, you will feel that no one can hear you. You have a voice, and you want to talk to someone in this world, but no one can hear you except a channeler or such kind of spiritual teacher.

On the contrary, you can hear what people are thinking about. It's very curious. No one can hear you, but you can hear the inner voices of every person. It's very curious. It's a first experience for you. When you were alive, you could hear their voice only when they spoke to you, but now, you can hear every voice of each person and inner person—a voice of just the thinking in the brain or in their heart or something like that.

But even if you want to reply, no one can hear what you want to say. This is the first confusion. So, you cannot leave this world for a week or 30 days or 50 days, usually. And, another type of people who don't believe in God and who don't believe in soul and who don't believe in afterlife will wander around their place, I mean their house or their company or their school or around there.

So, it's very inconvenient for you to be a ghost. You can hear everything from the living people, but you can convey nothing to them. Now, you are a ghost, so you can do nothing. If there were Ghostbusters, you will be pleased by meeting them. "Oh, Ghostbusters. Come on, come on, please help me," you can say like that, but no one can be Ghostbusters.

The only chance for you is to meet an exorcist. If the family you left goes to Happy Science shoja or branch, the branch chief or the shoja chief will exorcise with some kind of prayer. "I will say that all the evil spirits and strayed spirits should leave from your family," and "If it's an evil spirit, go to hell," or "Please aid us by sending an angel from heaven," or like that. It's not so comfortable for you. You, a ghost, want to be saved by Happy Science shoja, but the teachers of Happy Science shoja just want to save your family who are left and just want to dispel you. They don't think too much about you because you have no money. You cannot get their blessing. So, you must consider a lot, "What can I do?" You must think about that.

3

Reflection is the Most Important Teaching Regarding the Ghost Condition

Reflect on yourself through The modern Fourfold Path

Then, I'll teach you. Please start your reflection. If you belong to Happy Science organization or you are the followers of Happy Science, you once might have heard about our modern Fourfold Path. Number one is love. Number two is wisdom. Number three is reflection, and number four is progress. Just think about that.

Please think that, "Am I a man of love or not? Did I give a lot to other people, or only my family or only my colleague or like that? Or, did I just want to get love from other people?" Please think this first and remember what was the love you received from your parents or your husband or wife or your children or your teachers. Please think about that. And, have you done a lot to them in returning their love or not? This is the first point.

Next is about wisdom. "I believe in soul and God and afterlife, but is my life enough as such kind of people who believe in God or who believe in afterlife or who believe in soul? Am I honest or not?" Please think about that.

A computer is useless for a ghost

Then, this is the most important for your ghost condition. This is reflection, just reflection. Please think about where you should go. This is the main point of religion. We are just doing activities in this world, but these include your afterlife's destiny. I want to change your future. Nowadays, more than 50 percent of the population will go to hell, but also nowadays, the number of churches or temples is declining, and the people believing in God or Buddha are decreasing. Even the field of dead people is reduced and reborn into gigantic apartment-like great buildings of inhabitants.

So, you ghosts are just stray sheep. You can go nowhere, so you'll return to your home. After that, some of you, of course, will talk every day to your family, your husband or wife or children, and they feel something evil at that time, but they can do nothing for you because they cannot see you and they cannot reply to you. No one in this world officially can teach you in this condition.

Only religion or religious people can teach you. If your occupation in this world is quite opposite to that of religious people, you'll feel great difficulty in understanding. So, I've been recommending that even one book of mine will be a hint for you, the lay person, I mean the people who don't have enough knowledge or interest in religious matter.

Now, people believe in science and they think that science will resolve everything, but it is too much for science. Science can reveal only one percent of the universe. Scientists know almost nothing about our reality.

Some scientists have also a religious belief. It's OK, but scientists are usually bound to this world and the materialistic tools or machines, computers, or like that. But a computer cannot understand what is soul, what is another world, what is heaven and what is hell, so a computer is useless for the person who became a ghost already.

4

Three Points of "Life Reflection"

1) Animal-like appetite

This reflection is a little difficult for you, especially the people who have business in another area. So, please teach that kind of people, "When you die, please remember the following: One is your life, of course, this time. Was your life greedy or not, or have you been greedy or not? I mean, didn't you have too much greed in your life? Please think about that." You cannot understand what is greed, but I want to say that, if you live honestly, you can understand if you are greedy or not.

Or, please think, "Is there animal appetite after your death?" Do you have animal-like appetite or animal-like want, greed? If you think so, it's miserable as a human. To be human means to live thinking that, "I am a soul" and "I was made by God in the ancient age" and "This world is just a school for me to train my soul." This is the orthodoxical thinking of a religious person.

If you have lived animal-like, and after your death, if you feel animal appetite, it's very sad. I mean, in this context, animal appetite includes the sex-oriented attitude, and of course, the food-oriented attitude or money or some valuable things-oriented attitude, or just fear of something which is poisonous for you, or just to like the things which are good for you only. No spiritual value in that life. It's animal appetite. If you lose your body, you can do no animal-like activities. They are useless. So, you must be an existence beyond animal.

2) Anger

And, please reflect on your anger in your life. Your anger is really effective to the people who are following you, for example, if you are a teacher, sometimes you scold your students. Formally, sometimes, it's good. But in the common sense, if you want to get angry, it just means that you've lost your peace of mind and made some kind of difficulties in this world only. So, please see deep into your anger, and if you did too much, please reflect on that and want to change your anger into blessing others.

3) Materialistic thinking

And, the most difficult thing is, if you have a tendency of monopolism, I mean, the materialistic thinking only, you can find no materialistic-like thing in another world. You can see, of course, something. People are living in another world, and there can be seen a lot of buildings or houses. But in the true meaning, they are nothing. You can go through the houses and you can go through the bodies of other people because they also are ghosts. So, you can go through everything and you cannot grasp anything. At this time, you must recognize that this is the first experience, but the world is not materialistic.

Then, if you have received experience or influence from Karl Marx-like thinking, please abandon that kind of thinking and please believe in God and God's teaching. Even if you have been laughing at them, it's your mistake. So, please say, "I'm very sorry to you. I misunderstood you. I, myself, was bad, evil to you." This is very important.

But common people cannot change their attitude of mind, so I repeatedly have been teaching you that, "This world is not realistic, this is just a training room for you. Believe in God or Buddha. Another world is the real world, and you don't have any flesh-like bodies, indeed. So, don't have attachment to your bodies. You can be supplied, of course, by some supplement or food to survive in this world, but it's not everything. You can earn money, of course, but you cannot bring it to heaven or hell, either."

So, please think about if you are materialistic or not. Be spiritual. People who appear on TV usually laugh at such kind of people who believe in ghosts or who believe in God or believers of some kind of sect or so. Their appearances are quite different, but only one truth is in it.

This world is not the real one.
This is a false one or a disguised world,
So you are just experiencing this world.
And, of course,
You came from another world
And are reborn to this world,
And again depart this world
For another world.

And, where you should go is determined
By your deeds only.
What you did in this world
Will determine where you should go.

So, I've been saying that,
"Every day, do good things.
Every day, think that
This is the last time for you.
This is the only day for you.
Please live happily in the real meaning,
And say good things to others.
Or, like Santa Claus, you should be kind
To your children or other children."
These kinds of things are your reflection.

Improvement: "progress" of The Fourfold Path

And, improvement. "Is there any improvement in this world? While you have lived in this world, what did you do to this world? Was it a good thing that you lived in this world or not? Was this a bad thing for everyone or for God?" It's the value of your life. Please think about that.

What have you done in your life? Can you count that? For example, your business or your family or what you thought about and your influence on other people. I said these Fourfold Truths.

5

Spread This Truth to Have
All People Live Priceless Lives

After that, please believe in your guardian spirit and guiding spirit. Call them and ask them, "What should I do from now on?" They will say something, "Oh, you are destined to go to hell," or "Some kind of animal hell," or "Villain hell," or "Devil-like hell, black and evil and fearful hell," or "You can be a spiritual being and go to the next level, I mean the fifth dimension or more than that." Or, sometimes you will find that yourself is an angel. It's quite different.

But I just want to say,
"All you have learned in this life,
Especially learned by religion,
Happy Science books, will do
A good thing for you in your next lives."

This is the starting point of *dendo*.
So, please think that you are very priceless,
I mean you have a value in your life.
Please think
It's a great chance for you to live.

All I want to say is that,
"You are not destined to die tomorrow."
You have another day or another year to live.
You have enough time
To change your course of lives.
So, please think and believe my words
And spread this Truth to your neighbors
And to your country
And to the people of the world.
This is "The Ghost Condition."

Could you understand what I said? OK? If there
is any question, please ask me.

Q: How can we tell what type of spirit is influencing us?

QUESTIONER

Happy Science conducts various spiritual readings on paranormal phenomena, but most people don't understand what is influencing them. Is there a way to tell the difference between a ghost or space people or *ikiryo*—living spirit or animal spirit? How can we tell what is influencing us?

It's difficult to tell a ghost from ikiryo

RYUHO OKAWA

It's difficult. If they are just outsiders or not, if they are our followers or they want to be our teachers or lecturers, it's a professional way to understand that, but if they are lay people, to tell the differences of the ghosts is very difficult for them. So, at that time, please teach them that, "This is an important teaching from a heavenly existence," or "This is a bad example of the ghost phenomenon." Just make some kind of explanation only.

They cannot understand clearly about that. For example, to tell a real ghost from *ikiryo* is very difficult, even for me. Sometimes, I misunderstood it's a ghost, but it was an *ikiryo* that came from a living person. So, it's very difficult.

It's almost the same. I mean a ghost is an existence of energy. It's a thinking energy. Thinking energy is a ghost, itself, but in this context, a ghost is accompanied by posthumous or astral body of humankind. It's a surface of the soul, so it looks like as he or she lives.

But the real existence is not such kind of figure. It's like the light, itself. They are just shedding their light. It's some kind of plasma-like existence. So, even if the real person in this world sheds that kind of thinking energy, for example, to me, I sometimes misunderstand that, "Is it a ghost or the thinking of a real person?" and hearing them carefully, I will understand.

Their teachings tell who they are

Sometimes, *ikiryo* is the real thinking of the real person and his or her guardian spirit combined. If it is a higher spirit or not, it depends on the teachings only. Only the teachings can tell who they are. I mean, if you read some kind of spiritual saying or interview, and if you feel something good or something bad from them, it concludes who they are.

But when it comes to the Satan-like existences, common people cannot understand because they have very much experience and knowledge regarding how to control human beings.

For example, recently, we've found that Mao Tse-tung, the founder of the Communist Party of

China, is the largest devil of this Earth, and the Soviet Union founder or the leader of the Russian Revolution, I mean Lenin, and his successor Stalin are also devils. Oh, astonishing. And, in addition to that, their enemy, Adolf Hitler is also a devil. Oh! Incredible! Devil vs. devil was the real meaning of the Second World War. It's difficult. People are apt to think that one side is good and another side is evil, but sometimes evil vs. evil can happen in this world.

So, you must be careful about that. Even the famous people might not be angels, and someone who was seen as a small person could really be a great person. It really happens. And sometimes, the people who were murdered in this world, assassinated I mean, like Lincoln or Kennedy or Ryoma Sakamoto, or people like Shoin Yoshida or Hanpeita Takechi,* are miserable in this world only, but they left footprints of God or angels in this world.

Every day, every time is a teaching

So, it's very difficult to understand what kind of spirit it is. There need long time to judge. But you, yourself, can understand what you are in the near future, not so long future. So, if you are not a self-concentrated person and not a self-preservation-oriented person, you can understand what the spirit said is evil or good in the honest mind.

If you have greed or you are greedy, you cannot understand, and if you have too much confidence in you, and it's beyond what you can keep, you will be a *tengu*, a long-nose goblin-like existence. At that time, you cannot hear correctly the words

---

* Ryoma Sakamoto (1836~1867)
A Japanese revolutionary in the later years of the Edo period. He played a major role in overthrowing the *bakufu* (government) and starting the Meiji Restoration, including contribution to the establishment of the Satsuma-Choshu Alliance, but was assassinated by pro-government forces.

Shoin Yoshida (1830~1859)
A Japanese educator and revolutionary in the later years of the Edo period. From his private school were produced many key figures who played a leading role in overthrowing the government and in the Meiji Restoration, but was executed for political crimes.

Hanpeita Takechi (1829~1865)
A Japanese revolutionary in the later years of the Edo period. He temporary played a main role in the *sonno-joi* ("respect the emperor and expel the foreign people") movement in Kyoto, but was imprisoned following a coup, and committed *seppuku*.

from heaven or words from hell. So, be honest and obey God's teachings, and rely on your colleagues of the religious group.

There are a lot of mistakes which will be waiting you. But every day, every time is a teaching. You can find out what the truth is and what the spirit is and what kind of spirit it is. It's just the way to the professional leader of the religion.

So, there is no complete answer for you. Each effort will lead you to a greater position, and you can be a spiritual teacher. I think so.

Afterword

In simple words, your life is not limited to this world only. You have past life, present life, and future life.

Make efforts every day to return successfully to God or Buddha. Do not complain too much about worldly unhappiness regarding materials.

The kind of world that you see in your dreams is actually the real world.

When you are suffering a lot spiritually, just pray. First abandon worldly desires, and try to live a life of gratitude and giving back.

Ryuho Okawa
Master & CEO of Happy Science Group
Jan. 28, 2020

ABOUT THE AUTHOR

Founder and CEO of Happy Science Group.

Ryuho Okawa was born on July 7th 1956, in Tokushima, Japan. After graduating from the University of Tokyo with a law degree, he joined a Tokyo-based trading house. While working at its New York headquarters, he studied international finance at the Graduate Center of the City University of New York. In 1981, he attained Great Enlightenment and became aware that he is El Cantare with a mission to bring salvation to all humankind.

In 1986, he established Happy Science. It now has members in over 165 countries across the world, with more than 700 branches and temples as well as 10,000 missionary houses around the world.

He has given over 3,400 lectures (of which more than 150 are in English) and published over 3,000 books (of which more than 600 are Spiritual Interview Series), and many are translated into 40 languages. Along with *The Laws of the Sun* and *The Laws Of Messiah*, many of the books have become best sellers or million sellers. To date, Happy Science has produced 25 movies. The original story and original concept were given by the Executive Producer Ryuho Okawa. He has also composed music and written lyrics of over 450 pieces.

Moreover, he is the Founder of Happy Science University and Happy Science Academy (Junior and Senior High School), Founder and President of the Happiness Realization Party, Founder and Honorary Headmaster of Happy Science Institute of Government and Management, Founder of IRH Press Co., Ltd., and the Chairperson of NEW STAR PRODUCTION Co., Ltd. and ARI Production Co., Ltd.

WHAT IS EL CANTARE?

El Cantare means "the Light of the Earth," and is the Supreme God of the Earth who has been guiding humankind since the beginning of Genesis. He is whom Jesus called Father and Muhammad called Allah, and is *Ame-no-Mioya-Gami*, Japanese Father God. Different parts of El Cantare's core consciousness have descended to Earth in the past, once as Alpha and another as Elohim. His branch spirits, such as Shakyamuni Buddha and Hermes, have descended to Earth many times and helped to flourish many civilizations. To unite various religions and to integrate various fields of study in order to build a new civilization on Earth, a part of the core consciousness has descended to Earth as Master Ryuho Okawa.

Alpha is a part of the core consciousness of El Cantare who descended to Earth around 330 million years ago. Alpha preached Earth's Truths to harmonize and unify Earth-born humans and space people who came from other planets.

Elohim is a part of the core consciousness of El Cantare who descended to Earth around 150 million years ago. He gave wisdom, mainly on the differences of light and darkness, good and evil.

Ame-no-Mioya-Gami (Japanese Father God) is the Creator God and the Father God who appears in the ancient literature, *Hotsuma Tsutae*. It is believed that He descended on the foothills of Mt. Fuji about 30,000 years ago and built the Fuji dynasty, which is the root of the Japanese civilization. With justice as the central pillar, Ame-no-Mioya-Gami's teachings spread to ancient civilizations of other countries in the world.

Shakyamuni Buddha was born as a prince into the Shakya Clan in India around 2,600 years ago. When he was 29 years old, he renounced the world and sought enlightenment. He later attained Great Enlightenment and founded Buddhism.

Hermes is one of the 12 Olympian gods in Greek mythology, but the spiritual Truth is that he taught the teachings of love and progress around 4,300 years ago that became the origin of the current Western civilization. He is a hero that truly existed.

Ophealis was born in Greece around 6,500 years ago and was the leader who took an expedition to as far as Egypt. He is the God of miracles, prosperity, and arts, and is known as Osiris in the Egyptian mythology.

Rient Arl Croud was born as a king of the ancient Incan Empire around 7,000 years ago and taught about the mysteries of the mind. In the heavenly world, he is responsible for the interactions that take place between various planets.

Thoth was an almighty leader who built the golden age of the Atlantic civilization around 12,000 years ago. In the Egyptian mythology, he is known as god Thoth.

Ra Mu was a leader who built the golden age of the civilization of Mu around 17,000 years ago. As a religious leader and a politician, he ruled by uniting religion and politics.

ABOUT HAPPY SCIENCE

Happy Science is a global movement that empowers individuals to find purpose and spiritual happiness and to share that happiness with their families, societies, and the world. With more than twelve million members around the world, Happy Science aims to increase awareness of spiritual truths and expand our capacity for love, compassion, and joy so that together we can create the kind of world we all wish to live in.

Activities at Happy Science are based on the Principles of Happiness (Love, Wisdom, Self-Reflection, and Progress). These principles embrace worldwide philosophies and beliefs, transcending boundaries of culture and religions.

Love teaches us to give ourselves freely without expecting anything in return; it encompasses giving, nurturing, and forgiving.

Wisdom leads us to the insights of spiritual truths, and opens us to the true meaning of life and the will of God (the universe, the highest power, Buddha).

Self-Reflection brings a mindful, nonjudgmental lens to our thoughts and actions to help us find our truest selves—the essence of our souls—and deepen our connection to the highest power. It helps us attain a clean and peaceful mind and leads us to the right life path.

Progress emphasizes the positive, dynamic aspects of our spiritual growth—actions we can take to manifest and spread happiness around the world. It's a path that not only expands our soul growth, but also furthers the collective potential of the world we live in.

PROGRAMS AND EVENTS

The doors of Happy Science are open to all. We offer a variety of programs and events, including self-exploration and self-growth programs, spiritual seminars, meditation and contemplation sessions, study groups, and book events.

Our programs are designed to:
* Deepen your understanding of your purpose and meaning in life
* Improve your relationships and increase your capacity to love unconditionally
* Attain peace of mind, decrease anxiety and stress, and feel positive
* Gain deeper insights and a broader perspective on the world
* Learn how to overcome life's challenges
  ... and much more.

For more information, visit happy-science.org.

CONTACT INFORMATION

Happy Science is a worldwide organization with branches and temples around the globe. For a comprehensive list, visit the worldwide directory at *happy-science.org*. The following are some of the many Happy Science locations:

UNITED STATES AND CANADA

New York
79 Franklin St., New York, NY 10013, USA
Phone: 1-212-343-7972
Fax: 1-212-343-7973
Email: ny@happy-science.org
Website: happyscience-usa.org

New Jersey
66 Hudson St., #2R, Hoboken, NJ 07030, USA
Phone: 1-201-313-0127
Email: nj@happy-science.org
Website: happyscience-usa.org

Chicago
2300 Barrington Rd., Suite #400,
Hoffman Estates, IL 60169, USA
Phone: 1-630-937-3077
Email: chicago@happy-science.org
Website: happyscience-usa.org

Florida
5208 8th St., Zephyrhills, FL 33542, USA
Phone: 1-813-715-0000
Fax: 1-813-715-0010
Email: florida@happy-science.org
Website: happyscience-usa.org

Atlanta
1874 Piedmont Ave., NE Suite 360-C
Atlanta, GA 30324, USA
Phone: 1-404-892-7770
Email: atlanta@happy-science.org
Website: happyscience-usa.org

San Francisco
525 Clinton St. Redwood City, CA
94062, USA
Phone & Fax: 1-650-363-2777
Email: sf@happy-science.org
Website: happyscience-usa.org

Los Angeles
1590 E. Del Mar Blvd., Pasadena, CA
91106, USA
Phone: 1-626-395-7775
Fax: 1-626-395-7776
Email: la@happy-science.org
Website: happyscience-usa.org

Orange County
16541 Gothard St. Suite 104
Huntington Beach, CA 92647
Phone: 1-714-659-1501
Email: oc@happy-science.org
Website: happyscience-usa.org

San Diego
7841 Balboa Ave. Suite #202
San Diego, CA 92111, USA
Phone: 1-626-395-7775
Fax: 1-626-395-7776
E-mail: sandiego@happy-science.org
Website: happyscience-usa.org

Hawaii
Phone: 1-808-591-9772
Fax: 1-808-591-9776
Email: hi@happy-science.org
Website: happyscience-usa.org

Kauai
3343 Kanakolu Street, Suite 5
Lihue, HI 96766, USA
Phone: 1-808-822-7007
Fax: 1-808-822-6007
Email: kauai-hi@happy-science.org
Website: happyscience-usa.org

Toronto
845 The Queensway Etobicoke,
ON M8Z 1N6, Canada
Phone: 1-416-901-3747
Email: toronto@happy-science.org
Website: happy-science.ca

INTERNATIONAL

Tokyo
1-6-7 Togoshi, Shinagawa,
Tokyo, 142-0041, Japan
Phone: 81-3-6384-5770
Fax: 81-3-6384-5776
Email: tokyo@happy-science.org
Website: happy-science.org

London
3 Margaret St.London,
W1W 8RE United Kingdom
Phone: 44-20-7323-9255
Fax: 44-20-7323-9344
Email: eu@happy-science.org
Website: www.happyscience-uk.org

Sydney
516 Pacific Highway, Lane Cove North,
2066 NSW, Australia
Phone: 61-2-9411-2877
Fax: 61-2-9411-2822
Email: sydney@happy-science.org

Sao Paulo
Rua. Domingos de Morais 1154,
Vila Mariana, Sao Paulo SP
CEP 04010-100, Brazil
Phone: 55-11-5088-3800
Email: sp@happy-science.org
Website: happyscience.com.br

Jundiai
Rua Congo, 447, Jd. Bonfiglioli
Jundiai-CEP, 13207-340, Brazil
Phone: 55-11-4587-5952
Email: jundiai@happy-science.org

Vancouver
#201-2607 East 49th Avenue,
Vancouver, BC, V5S 1J9, Canada
Phone: 1-604-437-7735
Fax: 1-604-437-7764
Email: vancouver@happy-science.org
Website: happy-science.ca

Seoul
74, Sadang-ro 27-gil, Dongjak-gu,
Seoul, Korea
Phone: 82-2-3478-8777
Fax: 82-2-3478-9777
Email: korea@happy-science.org
Website: happyscience-korea.org

Taipei
No. 89, Lane 155, Dunhua N. Road,
Songshan District, Taipei City 105, Taiwan
Phone: 886-2-2719-9377
Fax: 886-2-2719-5570
Email: taiwan@happy-science.org
Website: happyscience-tw.org

Kuala Lumpur
No 22A, Block 2, Jalil Link Jalan Jalil
Jaya 2, Bukit Jalil 57000,
Kuala Lumpur, Malaysia
Phone: 60-3-8998-7877
Fax: 60-3-8998-7977
Email: malaysia@happy-science.org
Website: happyscience.org.my

Kathmandu
Kathmandu Metropolitan City,
Ward No. 15, Ring Road, Kimdol,
Sitapaila Kathmandu, Nepal
Phone: 977-1-427-2931
Email: nepal@happy-science.org

Kampala
Plot 877 Rubaga Road, Kampala
P.O. Box 34130 Kampala, UGANDA
Phone: 256-79-4682-121
Email: uganda@happy-science.org

ABOUT IRH PRESS

IRH Press Co., Ltd., based in Tokyo, was founded in 1987 as a publishing division of Happy Science. IRH Press publishes religious and spiritual books, journals, magazines and also operates broadcast and film production enterprises. For more information, visit *okawabooks.com*.

Follow us on:

Facebook: Okawa Books   Twitter: Okawa Books
Goodreads: Ryuho Okawa   Instagram: OkawaBooks
Pinterest: Okawa Books

RYUHO OKAWA'S LAWS SERIES

The Laws Series is an annual volume of books that are mainly comprised of Ryuho Okawa's lectures on various topics that highlight principles and guidelines for the activities of Happy Science every year. *The Laws of the Sun*, the first publication of the Laws Series, ranked in the annual best-selling list in Japan in 1994. Since then, all of the Laws Series' titles have ranked in the annual best-selling list for more than two decades, setting socio-cultural trends in Japan and around the world.

THE TRILOGY

The first three volumes of the Laws Series, *The Laws of the Sun*, *The Golden Laws*, and *The Nine Dimensions* make a trilogy that completes the basic framework of the teachings of God's Truths. *The Laws of the Sun* discusses the structure of God's Laws, *The Golden Laws* expounds on the doctrine of time, and *The Nine Dimensions* reveals the nature of space.

BOOKS BY RYUHO OKAWA

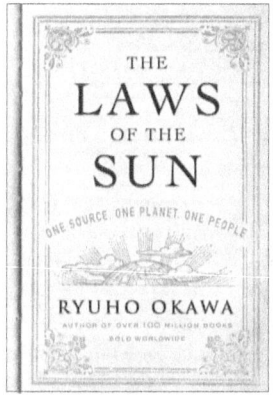

THE LAWS OF THE SUN
ONE SOURCE, ONE PLANET, ONE PEOPLE

Paperback • 288 pages • $15.95
ISBN: 978-1-942125-43-3

IMAGINE IF YOU COULD ASK GOD why He created this world and what spiritual laws He used to shape us—and everything around us. If we could understand His designs and intentions, we could discover what our goals in life should be and whether our actions move us closer to those goals or farther away.

At a young age, a spiritual calling prompted Ryuho Okawa to outline what he innately understood to be universal truths for all humankind. In The Laws of the Sun, Okawa outlines these laws of the universe and provides a road map for living one's life with greater purpose and meaning.

In this powerful book, Ryuho Okawa reveals the transcendent nature of consciousness and the secrets of our multidimensional universe and our place in it. By understanding the different stages of love and following the Buddhist Eightfold Path, he believes we can speed up our eternal process of development. The Laws of the Sun shows the way to realize true happiness—a happiness that continues from this world through the other.

THE GOLDEN LAWS

HISTORY THROUGH THE EYES OF THE ETERNAL BUDDHA

Paperback • 201 pages • $14.95
ISBN: 978-1-941779-81-1

Throughout history, Great Guiding Spirits of Light have been present on Earth in both the East and the West at crucial points in human history to further our spiritual development. *The Golden Laws* reveals how Divine Plan has been unfolding on Earth, and outlines 5,000 years of the secret history of humankind. Once we understand the true course of history, through past, present and into the future, we cannot help but become aware of the significance of our spiritual mission in the present age.

THE NINE DIMENSIONS

UNVEILING THE LAWS OF ETERNITY

Paperback • 168 pages • $15.95
ISBN: 978-0-982698-56-3

This book is a window into the mind of our loving God, who designed this world and the vast, wondrous world of our afterlife as a school with many levels through which our souls learn and grow. When the religions and cultures of the world discover the truth of their common spiritual origin, they will be inspired to accept their differences, come together under faith in God, and build an era of harmony and peaceful progress on Earth.

For a complete list of books, visit <u>okawabooks.com</u>

THE LAWS OF STEEL

LIVING A LIFE OF RESILIENCE,
CONFIDENCE AND PROSPERITY

Paperback • 264 pages • $16.95
ISBN: 978-1-942125-65-5

This book is a compilation of six lectures that Ryuho Okawa gave in 2018 and 2019, each containing passionate messages for us to open a brighter future. This powerful and inspiring book will not only show us the ways to achieve true happiness and prosperity, but also the ways to solve many global issues we now face.

THE HELL YOU NEVER KNEW

AND HOW TO AVOID GOING THERE

Paperback • 192 pages • $15.95
ISBN: 978-1-942125-52-5

From ancient times, people have been warned of the danger of falling to Hell. But does the world of Hell truly exist? If it does, what kind of people would go there? Through his spiritual abilities, Ryuho Okawa found out that Hell is only a small part of the vast Spirit World, yet more than half of the people today go there after they die.

MY JOURNEY THROUGH THE SPIRIT WORLD

A TRUE ACCOUNT OF MY EXPERIENCES OF
THE HEREAFTER

Paperback • 224 pages • $15.95
ISBN: 978-1-942125-41-9

What happens when we die? What is the afterworld like? Do heaven and hell really exist? In this book, Ryuho Okawa shares surprising facts such as that we visit the spirit world during sleep, that souls in the spirit world go to a school to learn about how to use their spiritual power, and that people continue to live in the same lifestyle as they did in this world.

For a complete list of books, visit okawabooks.com

HEALING FROM WITHIN

LIFE-CHANGING KEYS TO CALM,
SPIRITUAL, AND HEALTHY LIVING

Paperback • 206 pages • $15.95
ISBN: 978-1-942125-18-1

In this book, author Ryuho Okawa reveals the true
causes and remedies for various illnesses that modern
medicine doesn't know how to heal. The practical,
yet unique cures that this book offers for a variety of
medical conditions can help us stay on the path to
physical, mental, and spiritual wellbeing.

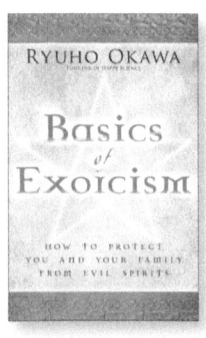

BASICS OF EXORCISM

HOW TO PROTECT YOU AND YOUR FAMILY
FROM EVIL SPIRITS

Paperback • 130 pages • $14.95
ISBN: 978-1-941779-34-7

No matter how much time progresses, demons are
real. Spiritual screen against curses – the truth of
exorcism as told by the author who possesses the six
great supernatural powers – The essence of exorcism
as a result of more than 5,000 rounds of exorcist
experience!

SPIRITUAL WORLD 101

A GUIDE TO A SPIRITUALLY HAPPY LIFE

Paperback • 184 pages • $14.95
ISBN: 978-1-941779-43-9

This book is a spiritual guidebook that will answer
all your questions about the spiritual world,with
illustrations and diagrams explaining about your
guardian spirit and the secrets of God and Buddha. By
reading this book, you will be able to understand the
true meaning of life and find happiness in everyday
life.

For a complete list of books, visit okawabooks.com

THE REASON WE ARE HERE

MAKE OUR POWERS TOGETHER TO REALIZE GOD'S
JUSTICE -CHINA ISSUE, GLOBAL WARMING, AND LGBT-

INCLUDING SPIRITUAL MESSAGES FROM GOD THOTH

Paperback • 215 pages • $14.95
ISBN: 978-1-943869-62-6

The main content is the lecture in Toronto, Canada
given in October 2019 by Ryuho Okawa. Also included
are his answers to the questions from renowned
activists who attended his lecture.

ON CARBON FOOTPRINTS REDUCING

WHY GRETA GETS ANGRY?

Paperback • 135 pages • $11.95
ISBN: 978-1-943869-59-6

Greta Thunberg, a 16-year-old environmental activist
from Sweden, gave a speech at the United Nations
Climate Actions Summit that shocked the world in
September 2019. In this book, Okawa summons the
spiritual beings who have influence on Greta, and has
them speak their true intention as to why they made
her say what she said.

SPIRITUAL MESSAGES FROM THE GUARDIAN SPIRIT OF AYATOLLAH KHAMENEI AND GENERAL SOLEIMANI

FOR THE MUTUAL UNDERSTANDING BETWEEN
IRAN AND THE U.S.

Paperback • 165 pages • $11.95
ISBN: 978-1-943869-63-3

In January 2020, while he was in Iraq. Only a day after
the U.S. forces killed Major General Soleimani by drone
attack, his spirit visited Okawa in Tokyo, and Chapter
1 is a record of the spiritual session. Chapter 2 is the
record of the spiritual session with the guardian spirit
of Ayatollah Khamenei who visited three days later.

For a complete list of books, visit okawabooks.com

THE NEW RESURRECTION
My Miraculous Story of Overcoming Illness and Death

THE ROYAL ROAD OF LIFE
Beginning Your Path of Inner Peace, Virtue, and a Life of Purpose

THE LAWS OF GREAT ENLIGHTENMENT
Always Walk with Buddha

I CAN
Discover Your Power Within

HONG KONG REVOLUTION
Spiritual Messages of the Guardian Spirits of Xi Jinping and Agnes Chow Ting

SPIRITUAL MESSAGES FROM OSCAR WILDE
Love, Beauty, and LGBT

THE STARTING POINT OF HAPPINESS
An Inspiring Guide to Positive Living with Faith, Love, and Courage

THE UNHAPPINESS SYNDROME
28 Habits of Unhappy People (and How to Change Them)

THINK BIG!
Be Positive and Be Brave to Achieve Your Dreams

For a complete list of books, visit okawabooks.com